GW00482000

Dummy!

Dummy!

Jim Greenhalf

STACK
BOOKS

Smokestack Books
1 Lake Terrace, Grewelthorpe,
Ripon HG4 3BU
e-mail: info@smokestack-books.co.uk
www.smokestack-books.co.uk

Poems copyright
Jim Greenhalf, 2021,
all rights reserved.

ISBN 9781838465384

Smokestack Books
is represented by
Inpress Ltd

'We don't live alone on this earth.
We are members of one body.
We are responsible for each other.
And I tell you that the time will soon come when,
if men will not learn that lesson,
then they will be taught it
in fire and blood and anguish.'

JB Priestley, *An Inspector Calls*

Contents

Before You Go in...

I would like to say that this collection was begun in uncertain times and reflects them; but that is only partly true. Some of the pieces go back to drafts from the mid-1980s and beyond. They did not have a future then: hopefully they have one now.

If they do that is due in part to the criticism, advice and encouragement of writers Peter Snow, Michael Stewart, Alan Whitaker and Andy Croft who brought out my first Smokestack collection, *Breakfast at Wetherspoons*, in 2018.

But above all, my love and thanks go to my companion Lesley, who helps me through.

Nobody Will be Reading What You Write

Thirty of forty years from where you are,
when those who know you are finally out of sight,
nobody will give a monkey's who you were;

fewer still will be reading what you write.
If you hope your scribbling will be remembered
it's a salutary thought to keep you up at night.

Those who affect indifference to get by
secretly hope another age will see the light
and future generations will explain just why.

When nobody understands a bloody word you write,
it's hard to tell yourself it doesn't matter and go on
trying, as you run out of lines to recite.

Harder still to see the unworthy gonged and flattered –
they won't vanish overnight,
unlike everything that you thought was true and mattered.

An inflated prostate displaces Dionysus;
but don't waste your time dying with the light,
wondering if anybody's reading what you left behind
when, finally, you are out of sight.

Not Bald Yet

Yes, Alexa, I could have made more of an effort
after the fatwa to make a splash in London.
My columns marched in triumph towards the prize;

but I lacked the moxie; too angry, too shy,
unwilling to network or compromise.
As soon as possible I took flight.

You had to be fast on your feet, quick of mouth
and thick of hide, for a life on the Fleet.
I couldn't see myself as Chapman Pincher

or Paul Foot, but was bold enough to sing
Mary Magdalene in Soho's Bathhouse
pub one summer night.

Though life makes us
tired, hairless and toothless,
I'm not bald yet and I can still bite.

We've always got the news to mislead us
as we slip between highchairs and wheelchairs
towards the exit.

Gone are the Days of the 34b

for Chris Massie after his wife Wendy lamented her bra size

Gone are the days of the 34b
and the Green Line bus
to leafy provinces.
My waistline, 38, was the same as the red
Routemaster to Victoria.
It is not what it was.
My XL factor multiplied by three
shows that, like the cosmos,
I too am expanding.
But to what end?

Everything is restless –
the mind, the heart;
even the trees
wave their arms like furious MPs.
As big as we may be,
something's gone missing.
I don't live in the past,
a friend said before leaving,
but the past lives in me.
Is that what we're feeling?

Where are we?
we ask one another,
unsure if the other is listening.
The branches of libraries
close like books.
The world is rolled
by spivs and crooks.
Gone are the days of the 34b
and the Green Line bus
to leafy provinces.

That Was the Year That Was

1967 must seem like heaven now.
There was plenty of work
to go to or shirk.
No bombs in cars,
just dynamite in skirts.

That was the year I met
Alfred Jarry and Jacques Prévert
in the local library.
When peace was love
and love was free for all
who could afford it.
That summer before
Kennedy and King were shot
and the napalm war.

That was the year
George Harrison's
gently weeping sitar,
and flock wallpaper arabesques
of a thousand provincial
Taj Mahals,
restored the dream
of the sacred cow
between Calcutta and Kabul.

That was the year
solicitors named Trevor,
unhappy with the Humber,
the wife, bank holiday air-shows,
worried about their daughters
playing house with roughs
from tenements and tower blocks
they hoped they'd left behind.
Roll on, roll off,

that was the year of
wild cats on railways,
in freight yards, the docks;
threats to the food supply
stored against the fear
of Strontium 90 fallout,
the unconscripted future.
That was the year
we did our thing

and knocked on wood,
the year the world
changed forever,
but not necessarily
for good.

Let them go, the years
you believe were the best:
Control Z will not bring them back.
Motion, like crime, resists arrest.

Songs for 21 Whittingstall Road, Fulham, 1969–1972

Burlesque,
much brass,
marching also,
a figure of clowns
looping.

Drumrolls,
side-winding flutes
frivolous, laughter
as the clowns
fool.

For Poulenc and Satie
and This Week's Composer,
sing ho,
for Holub and Hollo,
bubble baths,
and friends upstairs,
sing ho,
for simple things
sing ho.

Where is the life,
these winters, those summers?
The moon looks down on us.
Who is left to admire?

They came and went,
as they thought owing no words,
left without even saying
fuck you
for the lovely time we've had.
No, not even that.

Half-crazy with sadness,
boredom, fatigue,
with no one especial
to share my banana.
At two in the morning,
I try to keep faith.

If you have a journey to make
remember, the jokes
are against us.
And if ever you come
to an enchanted place:
sing ho
for simple things,
sing ho.

Figure in a Landscape

In a small London churchyard
by the banks of the Thames at Fulham,
I sometimes spied an ageless lady,
under the plane trees of evening.
She wore Italian widow's black,
but looked like an English spinster,
gliding between cobwebs and tombstones.
She shawled herself in shadow,
until the coast cleared of human traffic.
She seemed a stranger to the century,
with its Moon-shots and gunshots:
a refugee from another planet,
walled off from the madness.
Like a spider centred in silence,
she smiled among the dead
as she broke up bread from a bag,
to feed the birds discreetly.
I was afraid, half-fearing
she was mad-lonely who smiled
because she saw through me.

The Wish

How I wish I was intelligent,
the intelligent have all the luck;
even their ugliness is elegant:
things avoid them, we have to duck.

They're always surprised and indignant
when life does something unfair.
We stupidly accept it;
but one of them writes King Lear.

John Berryman's *77 Dream Songs*

I regret only the stale puns and self-pity
that punctuated my feverish attempts
to emulate what he had done:
to sound the bottom of the warring self's complaint
and gravely mock
the grim pursuit of happiness.

In spite of stylistic indulgences
that prize-winning drunks
and academics get away with,
his modern sonnets showed me
how I too might make my rosary
of knots and cruxes a rope.

The perpetrator of these conceits
escaped over the icy edge in 72:
fifty-eight, acclaimed and dead.
He fell a long way. At twenty-three,
I had farther to go, unknown, cold bones
under the ground of Downs Road, Hackney.

Leaving Bratislava

I came in through the front door by steam train from Prague
and three weeks later left by the back door,
Bratislava by bus to Vienna.
It was all one country in those days,
when I was young and believed in romantic love,
the excitement of passports and borders.

Now the map has changed, little is as it was before.
Only the Milky Way's fried eggs above Ulm
might look bigger to a hungry roadside hitcher.
The motorcyclist with a Marxist beard,
who scrambled me northwards,
and the Belgian soldier who drove me out of

West Germany: they cannot flip me back.
I thought my lucky days were a dead-end street.
The future I could not imagine in 1971
is where, by stages, I have come.
The road ahead that I could not see,
was all the time under my feet.

Old Christian Injunctions

To give and not to count the cost,
to fight and not to heed the wounds,
to toil and not to seek for rest,
to work and ask for no reward...

Old Christian injunctions
slide through my head
as the southbound train out of Leeds
picks up speed for King's Cross.

Prayers did not bother me
in the days of steam and diesel,
when carriage windows and doors
were not centrally locked.

Nor did mortal panic erupt
when the train inexplicably stopped
between Elland Road and Highbury.
Have I come so far only to be fearful?

Stillness increases with speed.
And so does wondering why
those coercive injunctions didn't die.
Football stadiums and churches on the left,

Eddie Stobarts on the roads,
a mountain ash the Brontes might have known
above Heptonstall.
Things have vanished or grown

like Peterborough, Grantham, Stevenage:
stations of the cross and moderately unhappy.
Tragedy, like the sea,
takes no account of biography.

arrival is still a surprise.
Looking out from the seventh floor
of a riverside hotel (its windows open)
for a skyline I might recognise.

Eyes of the Jackal

We walked across Pont Alexandre III
in the wake of Fred Zinnemann's cameras
tracking De Gaulle's black Citroen
on boulevards of art, revolution and resistance.
The day was as hot and blue.

Black-bearded face gleaming
on glossy covers of news magazines.
Americans had killed the Jackal Bin Laden,
now the world was waiting for evidence,
retaliation.

Outside the Quai d'Orsay
a solitary armed guard was waiting,
dreaming of his lunch,
his lover,
his pension.

The statue of Thomas Jefferson
was waiting, document in hand.
Not the Declaration of Independence,
nor even a writ for Habeas Corpus,
but a blueprint for his Virginia mansion.

We joined a queue outside a converted railway station,
a Manet retrospective, his stylistic incarnations –
this odalisque, that drummer boy, those 19th century
Bin Laden-bearded men of property –
they too seemed to be waiting.

In shady doorways, ladies with fake Algerian tans
in pursuit of life, liberty and happiness,
waited and watched as we crossed
shadowy squares to our back-water hotel,
the eyes of the Jackal upon us.

Waking up to a World in Crisis

I

Doctor, doctor, step outside the Tardis.
Tell me: should I stock up on vitamin D,
Manuka honey or Motown: Holland
and Barrett or Holland, Dozier, Holland?

Everyone's declaring we're in a crisis,
ever-ready to stretch
or self-dramatise misfortune,
the way a bookie lays off bets.

Is there something wrong with me?
In spite of storms, stress, and the chosen news,
my humour is only critical.
Is it gods making us mad, bad

and dangerous to know?
Or ourselves alone, sickening the roses,
driving Miss Daisy crazy?
Is it Ragnorak, doc, once again?

We're burning up, or going under:
which is it, and how should I behave,
before the old discontentment returns
as the world's chalk rainbows fade?

Should I raffle the house and car?
Or simply be more attentive?
In a crisis it is better to be
open-minded and inventive.

II

Love, I hear everywhere I go,
makes the difference.
Love gives us purpose when all else fails
or goes crazy.
Love is the sickness and the cure;
but listen, doc:

you can tell me about strokes and seizures,
you can diagnose clots in the blood;
you can bar-chart slumps and depressions
and conceit more dangerous than drugs;
you can describe the colour of money
and how it can stain us like mud;

but what I really want to know is this:
where can you get your hair cut in a crisis?

The Earth of the Cool

Everywhere people are on the march,
coalitions of differences
joining forces.
High time too, you may say.
Looking on, my feeling is:

if you must coalesce,
please don't leave a bloodier mess
than the one you're striving to redress.
Try to praise the mutilated world,
even as you try to change it.

Hard as it is for the angry to make heaven
on earth, if you must rise up,
try to find a sympathetic mind:
one that says *no* sometimes
instead of *yes*.

If you cannot save yourself or the planet,
at least be kind
or calm and do no harm to fools
like me who've spent too much or too little
time at school.

Fold up the times, put them away,
or use them to line the cat's litter-tray.
The earth of the cool's no place
for bleating,
nor intemperate over-heating.

Waste Disposal

I am asked daily to sponsor
a jaguar, an elephant,
a child drinking dirty water.

I am asked to consider the future,
of the children I do not have,
grandchildren, none of them either.

My loved ones, what of them when I'm gone?
They will carry on, I imagine,
minus the burden of me

to carry along the road to heaven.
An inexpensive cremation,
paid in advance or instalments,

will make everyone happy,
I am told, and I'm shown
pictures of people with perfect teeth

laughing on patios, handing out
bubbly in fluted glasses.
I could be this happy,

if I prepare my death
warrant in advance.
Then I am asked to consider

saving a donkey,
a rhinoceros, a country,
to make myself feel better

before I too turn the corner
to the future,
that has no sponsor.

The New Puritans

Should I conceal my copy
of *The House at Pooh Corner*?
Would opening it still be safe in Dudley,
West Bromwich or Wolverhampton,
after Black Country burghers
tried to proscribe Pooh and especially Piglet,
lest they offend the New Puritans?
The zeal of the righteous
against a pig and a bear,
with a taste for honey and poetry,
comes as no surprise.
Fear of offending has become an offence.
Why should Pooh
and his companions be spared?

Turn the pages of Jonson's *Bartholomew Fair*,
see the righteous in beards and hats
hatching plots to entrap.
They did not all volunteer for The Mayflower;
some of them are still here.
Fast-backwards through the ages
until we, sans history, faith and rationality,
swing happily from tree to tree,
or turn on the seashore to flap a final farewell flipper,
as we disappear into the sea.

A Cautionary Tale of the Horse

Born to suffer and to rise above
the eagle's talons, the laurels of the dove;
the challenge always: to be yourself
and no other, irrespective of who
aims the Walther or the Glock;
and to tell your truth, providing you know
that truth comes a long way after love
of liberty,
as Laocoön, the Trojan priest, found to his cost.
Beware of Greeks bearing gifts!

he said and struck the wooden horse with his spear.
Do not be taken in! This thing will kill us all!
But the citizens of Troy, sick
of slaughter, curfews and restrictions,
the dubious reasons of their leaders crying wolf,
stood aside while the man who tried to warn them
was arrested and charged with treason,
then garrotted with red tape sent by the gods.
That night the horse gave birth to Greeks,
who summoned back their ships, and the city was lost.

Cultural Wealth Distribution

I am the man who abandoned Alan Bennett
under a bus shelter in Armley
and laid down *The Social History of the Machine-gun*
outside the Bronte parsonage.

I ran Krzysztof Kieslowsky's *Blue, White* and *Red*
up a flagpole at Five Lane Ends
and gave away a history of the Blues
to the bearded and veiled of White Abbey.

My surplus wealth,
in the form of discs, cassettes,
paperbacks, hardbacks and dvds,
was cast upon the stones
of Moscow, Jericho and Little Germany.

The Unbearable Lightness of Being
too heavy to bear indefinitely,
I let go like a balloon
somewhere
between here and eternity.

The Grapes of Wrath,
Gone with the Wind
and the letters of Sylvia Plath,
redacted by her mother,
found their place
in trains, on buses,
outside the gates
of schools
and doors of local government offices.

I taxed myself
and redistributed
my cultural wealth.

And when my life sentence
between the sheets
has been served,
my vagabonds may turn up too
on unfamiliar streets,
in bus shelters and stations,
the doorways of tenantless shops,
like *A Streetcar Named Desire*
and the letters of Van Gogh.

Chained to a Wolf

Walking in the city,
searching for myself again,
I saw an old lover.

Oblivious to my distant eyes,
she scarcely looked at what she saw
in the retina of shop windows.

She had seen me naked,
I had felt her deepest hurt:
yet what did we know of each other?

Reflecting on the mutability
of vessels we call relationships,
I barely heard the consoling voice.

Why so sad and grave?
It was a brunette without a stitch,
smiling from a picture window.

I'm looking for someone I used to know,
I replied. *Dummy*, she said.
Look at me instead.

I should be modelling in Paris,
said a blonde with paintbrush lashes;
but like you I'm stuck in the sticks.

Hey, lover! snapped a black-haired beauty.
Lost your love? So what?
Surprise another!

Have a heart, I almost cried,
until I realised:
she hadn't got one.

You're chained to a wolf!
a redhead declared.
Don't let the past devour you.

With only a kiss I could
deliver you from this.
I stood transfixed. Then a whistle,

the wolf inside me snarled.
When I looked again
nobody was there.

A Withered Tree

I was angry with my friend,
but didn't have the guts to show it.
I kept it to myself for days
and hoped, somehow, he'd know it.

My friend, however, did not see;
he refused or was simply slow;
he did not say a bloody word,
which made my anger grow.

Then I got angry with myself
for my gutless, unbecoming folly.
And so, at last, I told my friend,
and said that I was sorry.

No longer angry with my friend,
once again he is my mate.
Trouble is, I can't forgive
myself: now it's me I hate.

Gustav Mahler at the Potting Shed

for Alan Whitaker

He entered the garden-centre restaurant with wife and grand-
children.
The dome of his forehead tanned as though by
Austrian sunshine. His glasses mirrored the summer lake
where he wrote his Resurrection Symphony.
Amused and bemused, his mind on something other
worldly, he looked surprised to see me,

back to the wall, my favoured position.
I can't explain why this encounter struck a chord -
the flowers, winter sunshine, words written or said.
Men of a certain age learn to understand
their places within... sometimes they are comfortable...
sometimes they are their own unwanted guests.

Why does happiness make the heart ache?
Although from outward forms we hope to stir
the passion and the life; lost among the years within.
I left him peering into a lake of pea-green soup.
Take care, my friend, we have old bodies
but young minds; for that we should rejoice.

The Lake

Like a battered concert grand,
it still augments the park
where I used rage and argue
with God. Old lake filled with green sky,
the darker shapes of thought.
If I could hang you up like a mirror
would I see and feel more deeply?
You bear your scummy burdens
with unconcern I envy.
All the paper-boats of humanity
drift to one end and stick.

A man watches his two little girls
scamper close to the edge
to cast their crusts.
The sun which makes them happy
plays upon me like remorse.
You, old backwater, survive
without such philosophy.
You reflect things as they are,
however the images change.
Only fools like me
ponder what each one means.

Under the Eaves

Thirty years the city has given him a living,
a reason for rising every morning.
Under the eaves of the Town Hall roof,
he seeks asylum from the office and the clock.
Times change but not for the better,
he mutters as he eats his lunchtime chop;
our lot is to weep and die.
He counts the stairs going down.
Afterwards, mint in mouth, a stroll
before resuming what feels like fate.
At twilight, starlings swirl and swoop
in pre-determined patterns, making him
think of freedom. A reflex of hope
on the 16.41 home. Roused by the last light
of the afternoon, he watches women
he can only dream of undressing,
remembering the buxom ones
for whom conversation was a prelude.
But all they do is talk and lie,
he says, getting off before his stop.

Old Jupiter

The easel in his front room
always had a canvas waiting.
When he wasn't painting
he walked the streets,
morning, evening and afternoon,
passing wanted posters for missing cats.
Cropped grey hair –
Bertolt Brecht or John Schlesinger –
old blue jeans, scuffed brown boots,
a waterproof, red or yellow,
a splash of colour against sandstone
darkened by weather,
haling anyone whose eyes
met his deep-sea fisherman's gaze.
I talk to anyone, he trumpeted in the village bakery,
where he liked to hold court every morning.
And then he started limping,
then he started falling.
An iron bed replaced his easel.
In the middle of winter he disappeared,
joining the list of missing cats.
Old Jupiter.

And He Sang a Song of Farewell

for Tony O'Callaghan and his late wife Angela

On the last night of the old year
I stood at the back of St Cuthbert's Church Hall.
My friend sang songs about Ireland: the fear

of famine; the flight across the water
to the promised land; lost loves, lost homes,
and for some the risk of an unstamped future.

On the eve of my friend's departure,
I sat in the hall of the First Martyrs,
wrapped in a coat against the old winter's cold.

He played and sang McAlpine's Fusiliers,
and, The Town I Loved So Well.
Stories of terrors, hopes and cheerful arrears

in the land of roadside shrines and plaster saints,
that green magnetic field of rocks and loughs;
where headaches and heart-breaks

are offered up, beyond the jet-planes
flying between heaven and hell.
And as he sang me a song of farewell,

On the Banks of the Royal Canal,
I wondered what I would be to myself, alone:
where was home for me?

He urged me to be a follower of the truth;
but in those days I was also a follower of Beverley,
Gillian and Alison, Susan, Sara and Ruth.

The unquiet longing to belong
and, as so many times before,
fearfulness of going over the hills beyond.

As we did the night he drove his small red car
through snow to Stranraer, through Ulster's unlit acres,
to his wife's family home in Donegal.

I learned that home is where you happen to be:
your own back yard, a cell of some sort,
or a place in the dark in the land of the free.

Man Behind the Times

You should have seen me in the park this morning,
reading Shakespeare, Donne and big Ben Jonson.
For an hour not even the owners of designer dogs

could yap away the peace I'd picked from the pages
of my old book. Nor the mothers who had shucked
more children than garden peas.

The world is full of violence, selfishness and fear.
The grey heron, attuned to something more purposeful,
waits in the weir ever hopeful of fish.

And I am happy to be behind the times,
not waiting for windows or doors to open;
I am not a lift that's stopped between floors.

I try not to add to prattle. I threw my mobile in the Thames
after wasting half a day trying to supply it with power.
Its last texting place among broken Nazi bombers,

John Donne's old boots, the roots of Plantagenet trees.
Those not on the way up must be on the way down.
Or stuck. I am not making plans.

Poems & Spanners

Man's a trouble to the woman
who chooses him.
She gives her heart, he does his best.
She hopes for a great joy:

he gives her poems for Christmas
and a set of spanners.
She fixes the sliding toilet seat
as she occasionally fixes him.

Like reason and wood they season with age.
Out of time, money and love
they make a home, a purpose, a future.
No need to linger in the basement of the past.

Time flies when the years are busy;
and the mistakes they make add up to words,
trying to mind the difference
between what is said and what is heard.

Ashes and Bones

The happiness of the world which spins
faster than the drum of a washing machine,
is hostage to the proper functioning
of fridge-freezers, kettles,
credit black lists, motorway mark-ups,
plasma screens and geezers
that are reliable.

I never wanted any of this.
Ownership was a boulder of worry
I never wanted on my shoulders.
I said *no* to American Express.
The world was small enough
to feed, clothe and accommodate me,
give me work, friends, a purpose.

I had a feeling for something
beyond me. That is all it was,
that is all that was ever due,
among the ashes and bones
of the century that saw me born:
the strength of the true,
a thorn among weeds and roses.

Why People Play Pianos in Railway Stations

If I could live up to my intentions,
I'd be as fatalistic as a Russian in 1943.
If you get punched in the face too often
and your expectations don't soften,
you won't depend on words to make your play.

When it all comes down to feelings,
healing's rare in little rooms with ceilings.
When the centre is imploding
and all around is fear and loathing,
the margin seems a better place to be.

Some choose bars because they're meaner,
others dream of halls and arenas;
but when life is all abrasions,
out of nowhere people you'll never know
sit down at pianos in railways stations

and calmly play.

Son of Man

Fattened with ashes
we stare at heaven,
marking the place
where our parents
lie buried.

O light that burns my blood.
I have seen the angel of plenty.
I have survived from once-rich cities.

He rose three times.
With whips and lashes
they beat him black.
The dogged sun
rises every day.

Bitter development.

View from the Bunker

We're down in the bunker
hands covering our ears
while the ones above ground
are pumping in fears.

We're down in the bunker
hands covering our eyes
out of sight of the big birds
crossing the skies.

We're down in the bunker
fingers fisting our mouths
too tense to breathe in
too scared to speak out.

They've emptied the streets
they've shuttered the stores
they've closed all the borders
they're passing new laws.

They're spacing us out
touching is banned
only thoughts are inclusive
and washing your hands.

What times are these
when it's almost a crime
to talk in the street
and laugh out of line.

I'm thinking life goes on
in spite of the news
vapour trails above me
are like watching a fuse.

Runnymede and Heathrow.
I'm lifting my eyes
making the most of this place
before it shuts down or dies.

We're bunkered in limbo
awaiting the time
when the invader's defeated
and occupation's a crime.

Don't talk of tomorrow
just hope for a blessing
a bluebird, a blackbird
in the place we are going.

VE Day and William Tyndale

The unholy fires of V1 and V2
that martyred London before my birth
have been subsumed. Now dragon's teeth bunting
celebrates VE, the day of victory.
Regatta-like loops of red, white and blue
in May morning sunshine.
From lamp post to lamp post
their vapour trail goes
along the length of the path of shades
to the chained gates of the United Reformed Church.
Outside its tall doors painted Prussian green,
I am sitting with William Tyndale,
under beeches, between river and railway.
He tells me that faith is the substance of things unseen.
A page-turning breeze sways the bunting
and brings the smell of bread and roses
westwards from the canal.
The periscope heads of Canada geese
spy out the horizon.
Under the boot-heel of occupation,
under the threat of lash or fire,
how do we carry on or even start,
unless love beyond conniving be printed
on the hard-drive of the heart?

Breaking Bread with Lazarus

One icy afternoon in January,
the world tilting on its axis, everywhere
banks bursting, blood over-flowing,
everything going to the devil,
I slumped in a corner of a Bradford restaurant
that no longer exists, watching the Bishop
of West Yorkshire and the Dales
try to cut into a chunky chicken burger
with a knife and fork.
It was my last experience of this kind of etiquette.
I picked up my bread and wolfed.

Me and the Communist Party of Southampton

prompted by the Smokestack Books anthology of Russian war poems: Russia is Burning.

I was always a fellow-traveller,
instinctively mistrustful
of causes and crowds;
but me and the Communist Party of Southampton
share one thing in common:
we know that a move
in a rightward direction
usually begins
with a step to the left.

Caught in a storm
that no one saw coming;
stuck on a train that's inexplicably
stopped between stations;
adrift on a ship
without navigation;
in this age of science, I'd like someone to tell me:
are we really at the mercy of forces
beyond anyone's ability to guess?

We live and learn, we tell one another;
but me and the Communist Party of Southampton
know that the oldest lesson
the world always forgets
comes from war
and heavyweight boxing:
a lurch in a rightward direction
invariably follows
a body-blow to the left.

A Game of Doms

for Andrew Pashley

Stay safe, people tell me.
I reply, *Stay sane.*
When madness of a kind is rife,
when people believe the very air
is infected with the invisible worm
that kills in the night,
I go down to the river
where a westerly breeze
blows the sunny
waters of the Aire
in helicopter patterns,
towards the weir.
They hope Atlantic salmon will leap over,
and lost souls won't jump in.

In this secluded bower,
watching couples and children
offering bits of broken bread
to wildlife they are forbidden to feed,
I have forgotten what it's like
to take a train to somewhere
I have never been.
I have forgotten what it's like
to stand in the middle of nowhere,
where waiting is an act of faith.
Waiting for the leaves to stir,
the cards to fall,
the sound of dominoes,
invisibly, somewhere,
smacking the table.

England

The roads are full of injunctions:
keep your distance;
stay home;
follow the arrows;
keep off the grass.

I can truly say
that keeping my distance
has been a lifelong preoccupation.
I'm always giving way.
And I've been off the grass
since Thunderclap Newman.
My last puff was with a girl called Marx.

Home is where my passport is.
I'm going to huddle up to it
in case the Home Office mistakes me
for Anthony Bryan or Giuseppe Conlon.

Keep left, say the signs.
Well, I'll do my best
to stay on the right side of the lines.

Your England

Ye are many, they are few.
Of course, in May 1940,
the reverse was true.

Since then the few
have become the many,
too many to please

and tease indefinitely.
Too many who will not do
as they're told.

Should you choose
to raise your voice,
you must mind your p's and q's,

in case your tongue
prompts nurse to come
and remind the many

that they are few,
and that where they stand
is not their land.

Restoring the Picture

That oil painting is in need of restoration.
Solvents will dissolve time's glazes of dirt, dust
and tallowed varnish; but will the squire in his tricorn hat,
and his wife with her hounds, look the same to us;
the silky sheen of their clothes, their china-white faces;
will we still feel the same about the house and its grounds,
designed by Adam and laid out by Brown?

Stripping away the surface only slightly risks revealing
what, for two centuries, was brushed over by a leaf
of Caribbean sugar-cane. The picture, in its frame
the colour of old, cold guineas, assures us
that this must be the best of all possible worlds,
a golden age of prosperity to look back on
when darker times, like this one, reign.

A View from the Clubhouse in September

A granite marker-stone shows I am
twenty-six miles from Speaker's Corner.
The news is bad, some say it could get worse.

Distant crumps that could be guns or thunder,
though the Glorious Twelfth is over,
thump in multiples beyond the greens and bunkers.

Sandhurst cadets or Aldershot artillery,
practising for some turkey-shoot to come?
Is that what Dover heard that Saturday,

on that first weekend in July 1916,
the overture to the Somme?
Guns crump but we are blown to smithereens.

Somebody coughs, everyone else takes cover.
After the morning's first cigarette,
the body politic is a man puffing an inhaler.

They talk of lockdown, unsure if they
are willing. A siren's distant blast,
as though buzz-bombs are on the way

along Heathrow flight-paths. No need for alarm:
they're merely sounding off at Broadmoor.
We'll all be candidates for the funny farm,

if this goes on much longer.
If we are barking, solitary and poor,
it makes me fearful, it makes me wonder

if, when life decides my fate is done,
they will get shot of me
in one of those brick-built barracks on the A30,
opposite Prince Edward's Bagshot estate.

Crazy John

A dismal morning of windy drizzle.
After buying a few things in the Co-op,
I sit outside the Terrace Café, under
a madly clapping awning,
reading the obituaries of John Hume.

Except at the end, when memory forgot him,
he kept his sense of timelessness.
Chain-smoking from one crisis to another;
for more than thirty years
he refused to let history
road-block his driven destiny;
in spite of nail-bombs and Armalites,
Guildford, Warrenpoint, Armagh
and Londonderry,
he held his nerve.

Though human and fearful,
he worked in the wake of four thousand funerals,
neither turning aside nor going back
on the road of ambush and detonation;
thinking the unthinkable,
talking to the enemy,
taking the flak.
Some thought he was a communist, crazy,
or both.

He was from that same mad constituency
as Lincoln and Martin Luther King,
swimming against the current of opinion.
Those who make a difference or go round the bend
find their place on a gable-end.

Pit the rage of reason
against the monuments of the fibrillating heart:
it all comes down to stepping-stones,
mile-stones, tombstones,
a blade of grass.

Long after Denis Healey pronounced the Troubles intractable,
a photographer snapped
Gerry Adams, Ian Paisley and John Hume,
round a table, together.
I captioned it:
Miracles do happen.

Though some may doubt or wonder at it now,
we could do with another
crazy John.

9 October 2020

Samsara

Jet planes will be crossing over Runnymede and Windsor;
the Thames will renew itself through six counties,
under the thirty-five bridges of London, to Gravesend;
bread will be baked and newspapers delivered as the sun rises;
the mountains of Albania will look much the same
from Corfu's coastal tavernas.
It is the end of the working week. A storm in the east
blows a whiff of municipally-cut grass
and the skanky street wang of ganja westward
over the city's green domes and grey domes,
bringing a premonition of rain
as Friday prayers go up
and the rushing of trains, arriving and departing,
comes down over the flowering walls
of backyards like mine.
And a breeze ripples blue hospital curtains,
where someone waits to go home
and, elsewhere under a coverlet,
eyes close that might not see morning.
Two lives crossing,
the sense of going on.

17 April 2021

Black Landings

They've got rid of Macduff,
old wooden fisher of the Moray Firth.
The size of a small coastal cottage,
built in Ramsay MacDonald's place of birth,

it used to be propped between timbers
on Burghead's Thomas Telford quay,
a beached leviathan from the days of
Black Landings when skippers,

stranded by quotas, tried to cod
fish-taxing customs men.
Curved planking streaked copper,
oily black, fungal green, as though its keel

had weathered poisonous waters,
to fish for lobster, crab and mackerel,
or rescue men singing on the wreckage
of a storm-broken, sinking trawler.

They've planked and painted it up
and put away the Macduff,
behind the heritage Pictish fortress
and the ugly distillery they need for jobs.

John Cooper Clarke

I

The last Friday of October
only feels like Doomsday,
going home from the birth-place
of Charlotte, Anne and Emily.
Looking north across Stony Ridge Road,
beyond Hope Hill,
down into the valley of the clueless,
is like the end of civilisation.
We used to think it was a bit of a lark;
nothing bad would last
longer than Bernard Manning
took to light up an Embassy and laugh,
in Manchester's badlands.

II

Hands, face and boomps-a-daisy.
Give us this day somebody to love,
and somebody else to blame.
John Cooper Clarke, John Cooper Clarke,
deliver us from ourselves,
remind us how to laugh.
Take courage! Anne Bronte's
last words to Charlotte go down the drain.
Roll out the barrel and then roll it back again.

But what if giant spiders in Ray Bans
have decided that the days of tea
and Grandma Wild's biscuits are over?

The moving finger types
as everything goes to the wall
and people go down on their knees,
from St Peter's to St Paul's.
Conspiracies are all the same:
torchlights in the dark.

III

The wind whirrs in my ears,
a racing cycle changing gears,
chasing Constable's clouds.

Out in the open, I say my prayer.
An empty provincial railway station,
the grounds of a locked chapel, will do.

No masquerade, nothing shared;
just life going on as it is supposed to.
Out in the open I feel less scared.

The Route

Just as countries need disparate liberties
to be free,
my personal biodiversity requires
pastime and good company;
and though I like my solitude,
the idea of being
the man in the iron mask indefinitely,
or a bread and water mendicant on Skellig Michael,
a Prozac and Hobnobs bum on Mount Baldy,
has less appeal, year by year.

Brian Jones dying at the age of twenty-six
prompted someone to quip that the Rolling Stone
had run out of runway.
After decades of giving no thought
to surgeries and hospitals,
the further along the Yellow Brick Road I go,
appointments for both increase.

Every time I walk away
is like winning a vote of confidence;
but I know, only shortens the route
to that final strip of blacktop,
over the rainbow.

Last Thoughts on Peter Sutcliffe

They came from Lancashire and beyond,
stag-nighters on the red-light piss, Ripper tourists,
kerb-crawling Garden Lane, slowing outside number six,
hoping to snipe a shot of Sutcliffe's missus,
Sonia, wild hair blowing as she pegged out washing
or stretched on a ladder, cleaning the windows
of the pale, detached, pebble-dashed, house.
I sometimes saw her doing one or the other,
a figure out of Strindberg or Sylvia Plath.
Telephoto journalists, hoping to frame her from the house
opposite that I was renting, were turned away.
Spying wasn't what I wanted press freedom to mean.

As for Sutcliffe, dead at seventy-four,
I never saw the point of keeping him officiously alive
nearly forty years, for killing thirteen women.
Tracking back-streets of reggae-playing pubs,
trying to trace who he was, almost did for my sanity.
Whenever Broadmoor tested its security system,
I thought of Sutcliffe in his comfy room, with his paintings,
Jaffa cakes and letters from adoring females.
I don't suppose many of those who loved old 'Pete'
gave much thought to the twenty-three children
his hammer and screw-driver had orphaned.

The Drowning Man

Ask me anything you like, he said, drink in hand,
his voice warm as a good dinner gravy.
Hotel lunchers glanced sideways at them.
Wasn't he once a famous public man,
another big fish caught out by the architect;
and wasn't she the actress who married him?
His wife smiled encouragingly across
the top of her glass at me.

At first sight I felt sorry for him, wife on arm,
treading water in the cold station forecourt,
waiting for somebody, from his party or publisher,
to haul them into the warmth of the North.
The job fell to me, sent to ask questions
about his memoirs and his fall.
If he, with his buoyant experience
of high political office, felt humiliated,
knowing that nobody else was waiting,
he did not show it. Who was likely to buy his book
or even read it? He knew better than I did
that his explanations were small beer, dud currency.

After it was over they returned by rail to London,
where he died of drink the following year.

Without Vodka, Without Complaining

While hoovering the bedroom curtains,
I heard a man say he would rather die like a dog in a ditch
than clot the body politic. Oh well, I thought,
easy enough to promise the earth
and leave the blood, fluff, tears and dead skin
for others to clean up.

And, looking out of the window, I thought
I would rather content myself as a cat,
sunning itself on a wheelie-bin,
without the compulsion to
pronounce or explain.

Cats have feelings, they tell you with their eyes;
they live without the comfort
of vodka stingers, lying or complaining.
Food, shelter, a place of safety,
is all they ask
from those who serve them –
staff.

It's a Crock Monsieur

Oh no, they've found another Earth.
Hotter than the hottest interior
of a cheese and ham toastie,
a-flood with rivers of molten lava.

For those with a passion for travel,
this hurtling lump of rock and fire
is only 156 trillion miles from
Tim Peake's Vostok, that capsule

blazing down the throat of the dark.
Gliese 486b was always there, tucked
behind the sun, like a foreboding,
an unknown cousin or step-brother.

Anxiety's knot of gas rises
through the floorboards of the soul,
disturbing what we think we stand
secure upon. If limitless space

is the mind of God, isn't this
freak show of narcissism
enough, without another Earth
for civilisation to get lost?

A Walk in the Park

I'm tired of being part of
a major historical event.
Before nine in the morning
I'm off the leash, out in my space,
bouncing the river bridge,
to the post office
for puzzles in the paper,
not the news.

Turning into the park,
a cold autumn morning.
All around me squatting men
and women thrusting;
on the roof of the Half Moon café
they're doing Zumba –
semaphore with invisible flags,
warning, perhaps, of things to come.
A reviewer said I should lighten up.
After all, the worse things get,
the gayer poets should be,
Yeats says in 'Lapis Lazuli.'

Well, I am moderately happy,
in spite of the news
and the pig's bladder of piss
strapped to my leg for thirteen months.
I get by and I am exercising too:
warming my hands
round a stand-about coffee,
watching pram-pushers and toy dog walkers –
one day dogs will design their owners –
circling the cricket field,
husbanded winter and summer
by Billy Ricketts.
Where Sir Learie Constantine
hit sixes into the Aire
and Jim Laker scored a century,
I used to practise falling over.

Why should I stand in the dock,
or sit in the park's stocks,
for not *frolicking* and *carolling*
across the wastelands of modernity,
chanting bloody haikus to Gaia?
I'll take my chances among the ghosts
of some simpler poetry.

There is a stately gravelled walk
the length of Titanic.
This is my Grand Place,
my Luxembourg Gardens,
where, in spring,
I shall sit for an hour,
out of the current of the times,
the sun on its high wire
between the Mill's brick chimney
and the Non-conformist clock-tower.

Parsnip Soup in the Rain

It's not chicken soup with barley that's warming my hands,
though the ills that my bags and bones are prone to
could do with a shot of Jewish Penicillin.
The medicine I'm sipping is Parsnip soup, cooked up by
Salts Mill chefs, served inside but eaten out of doors
in December rain, because of the laws of tiers.
Times were once good. The sky is light-edged

over railway lines, allotments and my house beyond.
I lose track of the thirty years that these old quarried blocks
of Yorkshire stone have sheltered and uplifted me,
and all the loves that a lifetime gained and lost.
Through the railings of the rain, empty trains slide by
like syringes for blood or vaccine. Better days will return,
some hope. Salvator Mundi keeps his fingers crossed

So What?

After this is over, Alexa,
if only you are left,
all else forgotten, bereft, rolled over,
do not forget

Mitsuko Uchida
poised like Mount Fuji
over the keyboard
opening of Beethoven's
Fourth Piano Concerto
at the Royal Albert Hall,

nor the wonder and beauty
of the Second Symphony
of anvil-chinned Finn
Jan Sibelius,
Sussana Malkki conducting
Frankfurt's Radio Symphony Orchestra.

And if troubled waters
should flow over the bridge
long after David Attenborough
has crossed the Styx
So What?

Miles Davis'
double-bass and trumpet,
contrive to stop,
temporarily,
Old Father Time's metronome –
that black crooked scythe.

Advice to a Dummy

Hope is the last thing that dies.
The world does not need more
dummies who think they are deserving.

If you expect a special place, a spotlight,
you are probably more of a mirror,
holding yourself up for others to admire.

Smash the glass. Don't expect a career;
abandon all hope of further or higher:
there are too many like you already.

Writing won't save you, words
will only make you bitter.
You are merely a mouth making faces

at yourself, another fish out of water.
Take the plunge: aspire to something better.

Before You Leave...

In the poem 'The Eyes of the Jackal', Fred Zinnemann is the American movie director who made the political thriller, *The Day of the Jackal*. 'The Earth of the Cool' quotes 'Try to praise the mutilated world' from Adam Jagajewski's post-9/11 poem in *The New Yorker*. 'Under the Eaves' is a revised version of two poems that first appeared in *Grassington's Reflex*, published in 2007 by the late David Tipton's Redbeck Press. In 'Man Behind the Times', the line 'The world is full of violence, selfishness and fear' is a quote from the late Pope John Paul II. William Tyndale was strangled and burned at the stake for the crime of translating the Bible into vernacular English in the 16th century. 'A Game of Doms' also refers to former Conservative Government advisor Dominic Cummings. Thunderclap Newman, the band, had a hit in 1969 called *Something in the Air*. Anthony Bryan is a British West Indian who was summarily incarcerated for being an illegal immigrant, despite having lived and worked in the UK for fifty years. Giuseppe Conlon was an Irish Roman Catholic man who died in prison after being falsely accused of being one of the Guildford pub IRA bombers in 1974. He, his son Gerry and seven others were later cleared of all charges. Ramsey Macdonald's place of birth referred to in Black Landings is Lossiemouth, near the city of Elgin. The line 'Ye are many, they are few', is from Shelley's poem 'The Mask of Anarchy'. The late Bernard Manning was a Manchester stand-up comedian who owned The Embassy Club. The politician in 'The Drowning Man' was the late 1950's Conservative Chancellor of the Exchequer Reginald Maudling. 'Me and the Communist Party of Southampton' echoes a line from Alexander Galich's poem 'Waltz Dedicated to the Regulations of Guard Duty' in the anthology *Russia is Burning*. 'Old Jupiter' refers to Saltaire artist Iain Morris who died aged 73 on 24 January 2021; it is also the name of a character in Jacques Prévert's film *Les Enfants Du Paradis*. I owe the phrase 'Prozac and Hobnobs' in 'The Route', to Peter Snow. In 'Parsnip Soup in the Rain', 'chicken soup with barley' is a reference to Arnold Wesker's 1956 play of the same name. But it is also, of course, a reference to the meal. *Salvator Mundi*, the Saviour of the World, is a painting of Christ attributed to Leonardo da Vinci. The line 'Times were once good' is from the last letter of society osteopath and portrait painter Dr Stephen Ward to journalist Tom Mangold. Mitsuko Uchida is a distinguished Japanese piano soloist.

The end is where we start from

TS Eliot,
Four Quartets